Hawthorn And Lavender; With Other Verses

William Ernest Henley

HAWTHORN
AND LAVENDER

With Other Verses, by

WILLIAM ERNEST HENLEY

*O, how shall summer's honey breath hold out
Against the wrackful siege of battering days?*
SHAKESPEARE

LONDON
Published by DAVID NUTT
at the Sign of the Phœnix
IN LONG ACRE
1906

Ask me not how they came,
These songs of love and death,
These dreams of a futile stage,
These thumb-nails seen in the street :
Ask me not how nor why,
But take them for your own,
Dear Wife of twenty years,
Knowing——O, who so well ?——
You it was made the man
That made these songs of love,
Death, and the trivial rest :
So that, your love elsewhere,
These songs, or bad or good——
How should they ever have been ?

WORTHING, *July* 31, 1901.

First Edition printed October 1901
Second Edition printed November 1901
Third Edition printed April 1906

Edinburgh: T. and A. CONSTABLE, Printers to His Majesty

CONTENTS

b

CONTENTS

CONTENTS

ix

London Types

x CONTENTS

Three Prologues

Epicedia

A

PROLOGUE

THESE to the glory and praise of the green land
That bred my women, and that holds my dead,
ENGLAND, and with her the strong broods that
      stand
Wherever her fighting lines are thrust or spread!
They call us proud?—Look at our English Rose!
Shedders of blood?—Where hath our own been
      spared?
Shopkeepers?—Our accompt the high GOD knows.
Close?—In our bounty half the world hath shared.
They hate us, and they envy? Envy and hate
Should drive them to the PIT'S edge?—Be it so!
That race is damned which misesteems its fate;
And this, in GOD'S good time, they all shall know,
      And know you too, you good green ENGLAND,
        then—
      Mother of mothering girls and governing
        men!

I

HAWTHORN AND LAVENDER

ENVOY

My songs were once of the sunrise:
  They shouted it over the bar;
First-footing the dawns, they flourished,
  And flamed with the morning star.

My songs are now of the sunset:
  Their brows are touched with light,
But their feet are lost in the shadows
  And wet with the dews of night.

Yet for the joy in their making
  Take them, O fond and true,
And for his sake who made them
  Let them be dear to You.

PRÆLUDIUM

Largo espressivo

IN sumptuous chords, and strange,
Through rich yet poignant harmonies :
Subtle and strong browns, reds
Magnificent with death and the pride of death,
Thin, clamant greens
And delicate yellows that exhaust
The exquisite chromatics of decay :
From ruining gardens, from reluctant woods—
Dear, multitudinously reluctant woods !—
And sering margents, forced
To be lean and bare and perished grace by grace,
And flower by flower discharmed,
Comes, to a purpose none,
Not even the Scorner, which is the Fool, can blink,
The dead-march of the year.

Dead things and dying ! Now the long-laboured
    soul
Listens, and pines. But never a note of hope

Sounds : whether in those high,
Transcending unisons of resignation
That speed the sovran sun,
As he goes southing, weakening, minishing,
Almighty in obedience ; or in those
Small, sorrowful colloquies
Of bronze and russet and gold,
Colour with colour, dying things with dead,
That break along this visual orchestra :
As in that other one, the audible,
Horn answers horn, hautboy and violin
Talk, and the 'cello calls the clarionet
And flute, and the poor heart is glad.
There is no hope in these—only despair.

Then, destiny in act, ensues
That most tremendous passage in the score :
When hangman rains and winds have wrought
Their worst, and, the brave lights gone down,
The low strings, the brute brass, the sullen drums
Sob, grovel, and curse themselves ·
Silent. . . .
          But on the spirit of Man
And on the heart of the World there falls

B

A strange, half-desperate peace :
A war-worn, militant, gray jubilance
In the unkind, implacable tyranny
Of Winter, the obscene,
Old, crapulous Regent, who in his loins—
O, who but feels he carries in his loins
The wild, sweet-blooded, wonderful harlot, Spring?

I

Low—low
Over a perishing after-glow,
A thin, red shred of moon
Trailed.   In the windless air
The poplars all ranked lean and chill.
The smell of winter loitered there,
And the Year's heart felt still.
Yet not so far away
Seemed the mad Spring,
But that, as lovers will,
I let my laughing heart go play,
As it had been a fond maid's frolicking ;
And, turning thrice the gold I 'd got,
In the good gloom
Solemnly wished me—what?
What, and with whom?

II

Moon of half-candied meres
And flurrying, fading snows ;
Moon of unkindly rains,
Wild skies, and troubled vanes ;
When the Norther snarls and bites,
And the lone moon walks a-cold,
And the lawns grizzle o' nights,
And wet fogs search the fold :
Here in this heart of mine
A dream that warms like wine,
A dream one other knows,
Moon of the roaring weirs
And the sip-sopping close,
     February Fill-Dyke,
Shapes like a royal rose—
     A red, red rose !

O, but the distance clears !
O, but the daylight grows !

Soon shall the pied wind-flowers
Babble of greening hours,
Primrose and daffodil
Yearn to a fathering sun,
The lark have all his will,
The thrush be never done,
And April, May, and June
Go to the same blythe tune
As this blythe dream of mine !
Moon when the crocus peers,
Moon when the violet blows,
        February Fair-Maid,
Haste, and let come the rose—
        Let come the rose !

III

The night dislimns, and breaks
    Like snows slow thawn ;
An evil wind awakes
    On lea and lawn ;
The low East quakes ; and hark !
Out of the kindless dark,
A fierce, protesting lark,
    High in the horror of dawn !

A shivering streak of light,
    A scurry of rain :
Bleak day from bleaker night
    Creeps pinched and fain ;
The old gloom thins and dies,
And in the wretched skies
A new gloom, sick to rise,
    Sprawls, like a thing in pain.

And yet, what matter—say!—
    The shuddering trees,
The Easter-stricken day,
    The sodden leas?
The good bird, wing and wing
With Time, finds heart to sing,
As he were hastening
    The swallow o'er the seas.

IV

It came with the year's first crocus
    In a world of winds and snows—
Because it would, because it must,
Because of life and time and lust;
And a year's first crocus served my turn
    As well as the year's first rose.

The March rack hurries and hectors,
    The March dust heaps and blows;
But the primrose flouts the daffodil,
And here's the patient violet still;
And the year's first crocus brought me luck,
    So hey for the year's first rose!

V

The good South-West on sea-worn wings
        Comes shepherding the good rain ;
The brave Sea breaks, and glooms, and swings,
        A weltering, glittering plain.

Sound, Sea of England, sound and shine,
        Blow, English Wind, amain,
Till in this old, gray heart of mine
        The Spring need wake again !

VI

In the red April dawn,
    In the wild April weather,
From brake and thicket and lawn
    The birds sing all together.

The look of the hoyden Spring
    Is pinched and shrewish and cold ;
But all together they sing
    Of a world that can never be old :

Of a world still young—still young !—
    Whose last word won't be said,
Nor her last song dreamed and sung,
    Till her last true lover 's dead !

VII

The April sky sags low and drear,
    The April winds blow cold,
The April rains fall gray and sheer,
    And yeanlings keep the fold.

But the rook has built, and the song-birds
      quire,
    And over the faded lea
The lark soars glorying, gyre on gyre,
    And he is the bird for me!

For he sings as if from his watchman's height
    He saw, this blighting day,
The far vales break into colour and light
    From the banners and arms of May.

VIII

Shadow and gleam on the Downland
    Under the low Spring sky,
Shadow and gleam in my spirit—
    Why?

A bird, in his nest rejoicing,
    Cheers and flatters and woos:
A fresh voice flutters my fancy—
    Whose?

And the humour of April frolics
    And bickers in blade and bough—
O, to meet for the primal kindness
    Now!

IX

The wind on the wold,
    With sea-scents and sea-dreams attended,
        Is wine!
The air is as gold
    In elixir—it takes so the splendid
        Sunshine!

O, the larks in the blue!
    How the song of them glitters, and glances,
        And gleams!
The old music sounds new—
    And it's O, the wild Spring, and his chances
        And dreams!

There's a lift in the blood—
    O, this gracious, and thirsting, and aching
        Unrest!
All life's at the bud,
    And my heart, full of April, is breaking
        My breast.

X

Deep in my gathering garden
    A gallant thrush has built;
And his quaverings on the stillness
    Like light made song are spilt.

They gleam, they glint, they sparkle,
    They glitter along the air,
Like the song of a sunbeam netted
    In a tangle of red-gold hair.

And I long, as I laugh and listen,
    For the angel-hour that shall bring
My part, pre-ordained and appointed,
    In the miracle of Spring.

XI

What doth the blackbird in the boughs
Sing all day to his nested spouse ?
What but the song of his old Mother-Earth,
In her mighty humour of lust and mirth?
' 'Love and God's will go wing and wing,
And as for death, is there any such thing?'—
In the shadow of death,
So, at the beck of the wizard Spring
The dear bird saith—
    So the bird saith !

Caught with us all in the nets of fate,
So the sweet wretch sings early and late ;
And, O my fairest, after all,
The heart of the World 's in his innocent call.
The will of the World 's with him wing and wing:—
'Life—life—life !   'Tis the sole great thing
This side of death,
Heart on heart in the wonder of Spring !'
So the bird saith—
    The wise bird saith !

XII

This world, all hoary
With song and story,
 . Rolls in a glory
      Of youth and mirth ;
Above and under
Clothed on with wonder,
Sunrise and thunder,
      And death and birth.
His broods befriending
With grace unending
And gifts transcending
    A god's at play,
Yet do his meetness
And sovran sweetness
Hold in the jocund purpose of May.

So take your pleasure,
And in full measure
Use of your treasure,
      When birds sing best !

For when heaven's bluest,
And earth feels newest,
And love longs truest,
      And takes not rest :
When winds blow cleanest,
And seas roll sheenest,
And lawns lie greenest :
      Then, night and day,
Dear life counts dearest,
And God walks nearest
To them that praise Him, praising His May.

D

XIII

I talked one midnight with the jolly ghost
Of a gray ancestor, Tom Heywood hight;
And, 'Here's,' says he, his old heart liquor-lifted—
'Here's how we did when Gloriana shone:'

All in a garden green
　　　Thrushes were singing;
Red rose and white between,
　　　Lilies were springing;
It was the merry May;
　　　Yet sang my Lady:—
'Nay, Sweet, now nay, now nay!
　　　I am not ready.'

Then to a pleasant shade
　　　I did invite her:
All things a concert made,
　　　For to delight her;

Under, the grass was gay ;
   Yet sang my Lady :—
'Nay, Sweet, now nay, now nay !
   I am not ready.'

XIV

Why do you linger and loiter, O most sweet?
Why do you falter and delay,
Now that the insolent, high-blooded May
Comes greeting and to greet?
Comes with her instant summonings to stray
Down the green, antient way—
The leafy, still, rose-haunted, eye-proof street!—
Where true lovers each other may entreat,
Ere the gold hair turn gray?
Entreat, and fleet
Life gaudily, and so play out their play,
Even with the triumphing May—
The young-eyed, smiling, irresistible May!

Why do you loiter and linger, O most dear?
Why do you dream and palter and stay,
When every dawn, that rushes up the bay,
Brings nearer, and more near,
The Terror, the Discomforter, whose prey,

Belovèd, we must be ?   Nor prayer, nor tear,
Lets his arraignment ; but we disappear,
What time the gold turns gray,
Into the sheer,
Blind gulfs unglutted of mere Yesterday,
With the unlingering May—
The good, fulfilling, irresponsible May !

xv

Come where my Lady lies,
Sleeping down the golden hours !
Cover her with flowers.

Bluebells from the clearings,
    Flag-flowers from the rills,
Wildings from the lush hedgerows,
    Delicate daffodils,
Sweetlings from the formal plots,
    Bloomkins from the bowers—
Heap them round her where she sleeps,
    Cover her with flowers !

Sweet-pea and pansy,
    Red hawthorn and white ;
Gilliflowers—like praising souls ;
    Lilies—lamps of light :

Nurselings of what happy winds,
    Suns, and stars, and showers !
Joylets good to see and smell—
    Cover her with flowers !

Like to sky-born shadows
    Mirrored on a stream,
Let their odours meet and mix
    And waver through her dream !
Last, the crowded sweetness
    Slumber overpowers,
And she feels the lips she loves
    Craving through the flowers !

XVI

The west a glory of green and red and gold,
The magical drifts to north and eastward rolled,
The shining sands, the still, transfigured sea,
The wind so light it scarce begins to be,
As these long days unfold a flower, unfold
      Life's rose in me.

Life's rose—life's rose!   Red at my heart it
    glows—
Glows and is glad, as in some quiet close
The sun's spoiled darlings their gay life renew!
Only, the clement rain, the mothering dew,
Daytide and night, all things that make the rose,
      Are you, dear—you!

XVII

Look down, dear eyes, look down,
    Lest you betray her gladness.
Dear brows, do naught but frown,
    Lest men miscall my madness.

Come not, dear hands, so near,
    Lest all besides come nearer.
Dear heart, hold me less dear,
    Lest time hold nothing dearer.

Keep me, dear lips, O, keep
    The great last word unspoken,
Lest other eyes go weep,
    And other lives lie broken !

E

XVIII

Poplar and lime and chestnut
    Meet in a living screen ;
And there the winds and the sunbeams keep
    A revel of gold and green.

O, the green dreams and the golden,
    The golden thoughts and green,
This green and golden end of May
    My lover and me between !

XIX

Hither, this solemn eventide,
All flushed and mystical and blue,
When the late bird sings
And sweet-breathed garden-ghosts walk sudden
    and wide,
Hesper, that bringeth all good things,
Brings me a dream of you.
And in my heart, dear heart, it comes and goes,
Even as the south wind lingers and falls and blows,
Even as the south wind sighs and tarries and
    streams,
Among the living leaves about and round ;
With a still, soothing sound,
As of a multitude of dreams
Of love, and the longing of love, and love's
    delight,
Thronging, ten thousand deep,
Into the uncreating Night,
With semblances and shadows to fulfil,
Amaze, and thrill
The strange, dispeopled silences of Sleep.

XX

After the grim daylight,
Night—
Night and the stars and the sea !
Only the sea, and the stars
And the star-shown sails and spars—
Naught else in the night for me !

Over the northern height,
Light—
Light and the dawn of a day
With nothing for me but a breast
Laboured with love's unrest,
And the irk of an idle May !

XXI

Love, which is lust, is the Lamp in the Tomb.
Love, which is lust, is the Call from the Gloom.

Love, which is lust, is the Main of Desire.
Love, which is lust, is the Centric Fire.

So man and woman will keep their trust,
Till the very Springs of the Sea run dust.

Yea, each with the other will lose and win,
Till the very Sides of the Grave fall in.

For the strife of Love's the abysmal strife,
And the word of Love is the Word of Life.

And they that go with the Word unsaid,
Though they seem of the living, are damned
    and dead.

XXII

Between the dusk of a summer night
    And the dawn of a summer day,
We caught at a mood as it passed in flight,
    And we bade it stoop and stay.
And what with the dawn of night began
    With the dusk of day was done ;
For that is the way of woman and man,
    When a hazard has made them one.

Arc upon arc, from shade to shine,
    The World went thundering free ;
And what was his errand but hers and mine—
    The lords of him, I and she ?
O, it 's die we must, but it 's live we can,
    And the marvel of earth and sun
Is all for the joy of woman and man
    And the longing that makes them one.

XXIII

I took a hansom on to-day
    For a round I used to know—
That I used to take for a woman's sake
    In a fever of to-and-fro.

There were the landmarks one and all—
    What did they stand to show?
Street and square and river were there—
    Where was the antient woe?

Never a hint of a challenging hope
    Nor a hope laid sick and low,
But a longing dead as its kindred sped
    A thousand years ago !

XXIV

Only a freakish wisp of hair?—
Nay, but its wildest, its most frolic whorl
Stands for a slim, enamoured, sweet-fleshed girl!
And so, a tangle of dream and charm and fun,
Its every crook a promise and a snare,
Its every dowle, or genially gadding
Or crisply curled,
Heartening and madding,
Empales a novel and peculiar world
Of right, essential fantasies,
And shining acts as yet undone,
But in these wonder-working days
Soon, soon to ask our sovran Lord, the Sun,
For countenance and praise,
As of the best his storying eye hath seen,
And his vast memory can parallel,
Among the darling victories—
Beneficent, beautiful, inexpressible—
Of life on time!—
                        Yet have they flashed and been

In millions, since 'twas his to bring
The heaven-creating Spring,
An angel of adventure and delight,
In all her beauty and all her strength and worth,
With her great guerdons of romance and spright,
And those high needs that fill the flesh with might,
Home to the citizens of this good, green earth.

Poor souls—they have but time and place
To play their transient little play
And sing their singular little song,
Ere they are rushed away
Into the antient, undisclosing Night ;
And none is left to tell of the clear eyes
That filled them with God's grace,
And turned the iron skies to skies of gold !
None ; but the sweetest She herself grows old—
Grows old, and dies ;
And, but for such a lovely snatch of hair
As this, none—none could guess, or know
That She was kind and fair,
And he had nights and days beyond compare—
How many dusty and silent years ago !

F

XXV

This is the moon of roses,
　　The lovely and flowerful time ;
And, as white roses climb the wall,
　　Your dreams about me climb.

This is the moon of roses,
　　Glad and golden and blue ;
And, as red roses drink of the sun,
　　My dreams they drink of you.

This is the moon of roses !
　　The cherishing South-West blows,
And life, dear heart, for me and you,
　　O, life's a rejoicing rose.

XXVI

June, and a warm, sweet rain ;
    June, and the call of a bird :
To a lover in pain
      What lovelier word ?

Two of each other fain
    Happily heart on heart :
So in the wind and rain
      Spring bears his part !

O, to be heart on heart
    One with the warm June rain,
God with us from the start,
      And no more pain !

XXVII

It was a bowl of roses :
    There in the light they lay,
Languishing, glorying, glowing
    Their life away.

And the soul of them rose like a presence,
    Into me crept and grew,
And filled me with something—some one—
    O, was it you?

XXVIII

Your feet as glad
And light as a dove's homing wings, you
     came—
Came with your sweets to fill my hands,
My sense with your perfume.

We closed with lips
Grown weary and fain with longing from
     afar,
The while your grave, enamoured eyes
Drank down the dream in mine.

Till the great need
So lovely and so instant grew, it seemed
The embodied Spirit of the Spring
Hung at me, heart on heart.

XXIX

A world of leafage murmurous and a-twinkle;
The green, delicious plenitude of June;
Love and laughter and song
The blue day long
Going to the same glad, golden tune—
The same glad tune!

Clouds on the dim, delighting skies a-sprinkle;
Poplars black in the wake of a setting moon;
Love and languor and sleep
And the star-sown deep
Going to the same good, golden tune—
The same good tune!

xxx

I send you roses—red, like love,
    And white, like death, sweet friend:
Born in your bosom to rejoice,
    Languish, and droop, and end.

If the white roses tell of death,
    Let the red roses mend
The talk with true stories of love
    Unchanging till the end.

Red and white roses, love and death—
    What else is left to send?
For what is life but love, the means,
    And death, true Wife, the end?

XXXI

These glad, these great, these goodly days
Bewildering hope, outrunning praise,
    The Earth, renewed by the great Sun's longing,
Utters her joy in a million ways!

What is there left, sweet Soul and true—
What, for us and our dream to do?
    What but to take this mighty Summer
As it were made for me and you?

Take it and live it beam by beam,
Motes of light on a gleaming stream,
    Glare by glare and glory on glory
Through to the ash of this flaming dream!

XXXII

The downs, like uplands in Eden,
    Gleam in an afterglow
Like a rose-world ruining earthwards—
    Mystical, wistful, slow !

Near and afar in the leafage,
    That last glad call to the nest !
And the thought of you hangs and triumphs
    With Hesper low in the west!

Till the song and the light and the colour,
    The passion of earth and sky,
Are blent in a rapture of boding
    Of the death we should one day die.

XXXIII

The time of the silence
Of birds is upon us :
Rust in the chestnut leaf,
Dust in the stubble :
The turn of the Year
And the call to decay.

Stately and splendid,
The Summer passes :
Sad with satiety,
Sick with fulfilment ;
Spent and consumed,
But august till the end.

By wilting hedgerows
And white-hot highways,
Bearing its memories
Even as a burden,
The tired heart plods
For a place of rest.

XXXIV

There was no kiss that day?
No intimate Yea-and-Nay,
No sweets in hand, no tender, lingering touch?
None of those desperate, exquisite caresses,
So instant—O, so brief!—and yet so much,
The thought of the swiftest lifts and blesses?
Nor any one of those great royal words,
Those sovran privacies of speech,
Frank as the call of April birds,
That, whispered, live a life of gold
Among the heart's still sainted memories,
And irk, and thrill, and ravish, and beseech,
Even when the dream of dreams in death's a-
      cold?
No, there was none of these,
Dear one, and yet——
O, eyes on eyes!   O, voices breaking still,
For all the watchful will,
Into a kinder kindness than seemed due
From you to me, and me to you!

And that hot-eyed, close-throated, blind regret
Of woman and man baulked and debarred the
    · blue !—
No kiss—no kiss that day?
Nay, rather, though we seemed to wear the rue,
Sweet friend, how many, and how goodly—say !

XXXV

Sing to me, sing, and sing again,
    My glad, great-throated nightingale :
Sing, as the good sun through the rain—
    Sing, as the home-wind in the sail !

Sing to me life, and toil, and time,
    O bugle of dawn, O flute of rest !
Sing, and once more, as in the prime,
    There shall be naught but seems the best.

And sing me at the last of love :
    Sing that old magic of the May,
That makes the great world laugh and move
    As lightly as our dream to-day !

XXXVI

We sat late, late—talking of many things.
He told me of his grief, and, in the telling,
The gist of his tale showed to me, rhymed, like this.

It came, the news, like a fire in the night,
    That life and its best were done;
And there was never so dazed a wretch
    In the beat of the living sun.

I read the news, and the terms of the news
    Reeled random round my brain
Like the senseless, tedious buzzle and boom
    Of a bluefly in the pane.

So I went for the news to the house of the news,
    But the words were left unsaid,
For the face of the house was blank with blinds,
    And I knew that she was dead.

XXXVII

'Twas in a world of living leaves
That we two reaped and bound our sheaves :
They were of white roses and red,
And in the scything they were dead.

Now the high Autumn flames afield,
And what is all his golden yield
To that we took, and sheaved, and bound
In the green dusk that gladdened round?

Yet must the memory grieve and ache
Of that we did for dear love's sake,
But may no more under the sun,
Being, like our summer, spent and done.

XXXVIII

Since those we love and those we hate,
With all things mean and all things great,
Pass in a desperate disarray
Over the hills and far away:

It must be, Dear, that, late or soon,
Out of the ken of the watching moon,
We shall abscond with Yesterday
Over the hills and far away.

What does it matter?   As I deem,
We shall but follow as brave a dream
As ever smiled a wanton May
Over the hills and far away.

We shall remember, and, in pride,
Fare forth, fulfilled and satisfied,
Into the land of Ever-and-Aye,
Over the hills and far away.

XXXIX

These were the woods of wonder
    We found so close and boon,
When the bride-month in her beauty
    Lay mouth to mouth with June.

November, the old, lean widow,
    Sniffs, and snivels, and shrills,
And the bowers are all dismantled,
    And the long grass wets and chills ;

And I hate these dismal dawnings,
    These miserable even-ends,
These orts, and rags, and heeltaps—
    This dream of being merely friends.

H

XL

'Dearest, when I am dead,
　　Make one last song for me :
Sing what I would have said—
　　Righting life's wrong for me.

'Tell them how, early and late,
　　Glad ran the days with me,
Seeing how goodly and great,
　　Love, were your ways with me.'

XLI

Dear hands, so many times so much
    When the spent year was green and prime,
Come, take your fill, and touch
    This one poor time.

Dear lips, that could not leave unsaid
    One sweet-souled syllable of delight,
Once more—and be as dead
    In the dead night.

Dear eyes, so fond to read in mine
    The message of our counted years,
Look your proud last, nor shine
    Through tears—through tears.

XLII

When, in what other life,
Where in what old, spent star,
Systems ago, dead vastitudes afar,
Were we two bird and bough, or man and wife?
Or wave and spar?
Or I the beating sea, and you the bar
On which it breaks?   I know not, I!
But this, O this, my Very Dear, I know:
Your voice awakes old echoes in my heart;
And things I say to you now are said once more;
And, Sweet, when we two part,
I feel I have seen you falter and linger so,
So hesitate, and turn, and cling—yet go,
As once in some immemorable Before,
Once on some fortunate yet thrice-blasted shore.
Was it for good?
O, these poor eyes are wet;
And yet, O, yet,
Now that we know, I would not, if I could,
Forget.

XLIII

The rain and the wind, the wind and the rain—
    They are with us like a disease :
They worry the heart, they work the brain,
As they shoulder and clutch at the shrieking pane,
    And savage the helpless trees.

What does it profit a man to know
    These tattered and tumbling skies
A million stately stars will show,
And the ruining grace of the after-glow
    And the rush of the wild sunrise?

Ever the rain—the rain and the wind !
    Come, hunch with me over the fire,
Dream of the dreams that leered and grinned,
Ere the blood of the Year got chilled and thinned,
    And the death came on desire !

XLIV

He made this gracious Earth a hell
With Love and Drink.   I cannot tell
Of which he died.   But Death was well.

Will I die of drink?
        Why not?
Won't I pause and think?
        —What?
Why in seeming wise
        Waste your breath?
Everybody dies—
        And of death!

Youth—if you find it 's youth
        Too late?
Truth—and the back of truth?
        Straight,
Be it love or liquor,
        What 's the odds,
So it slide you quicker
        To the gods?

XLV

O, these long nights of days !
All the year's baseness in the ways,
All the year's wretchedness in the skies ;
While on the blind, disheartened sea
A tramp-wind plies
Cringingly and dejectedly !
And rain and darkness, mist and mud,
They cling, they close, they sneak into the blood,
They crawl and crowd upon the brain :
Till in a dull, dense monotone of pain
The past is found a kind of maze,
At whose every coign and crook,
Broad angle and privy nook,
There waits a hooded Memory,
Sad, yet with strange, bright, unreproaching eyes.

XLVI

In Shoreham River, hurrying down
To the live sea,
By working, marrying, breeding Shoreham Town,
Breaking the sunset's wistful and solemn dream,
An old, black rotter of a boat
Past service to the labouring, tumbling flote,
Lay stranded in mid-stream :
With a horrid list, a frightening lapse from the
        line,
That made me think of legs and a broken spine :
Soon, all-too soon,
Ungainly and forlorn to lie
Full in the eye
Of the cynical, discomfortable moon
That, as I looked, stared from the fading sky,
A clown's face flour'd for work.   And by and by
The wide-winged sunset wanned and waned ;
The lean night-wind crept westward, chilling and
        sighing ;
The poor old hulk remained,

Stuck helpless in mid-ebb.   And I knew why—
Why, as I looked, my heart felt crying.[1]
For, as I looked, the good green earth seemed
    dying—
Dying or dead ;
And, as I looked on the old boat, I said :—
'*Dear God, it's I !*'

[1] *At two years old, my child, being chidden, found this striking phrase.—W. E. H.*

I

XLVII

Come by my bed,
What time the gray ghost shrieks and flies ;
Take in your hands my head,
And look, O look, into my failing eyes ;
And, by God's grace,
Even as He sunders body and breath,
The shadow of your face
Shall pass with me into the run
Of the Beyond, and I shall keep and save
Your beauty, as it used to be,
An absolute part of me,
Lying there, dead and done,
Far from the sovran bounty of the sun,
Down in the grisly colonies of the Grave.

XLVIII

Gray hills, gray skies, gray lights,
And still, gray sea—
O fond, O fair,
The Mays that were,
When the wild days and wilder nights
Made it like heaven to be !

Gray head, gray heart, gray dreams—
O, breath by breath,
Night-tide and day
Lapse gentle and gray,
As to a murmur of tired streams,
Into the haze of death.

XLIX

Silence, loneliness, darkness—
      These, and of these my fill,
While God in the rush of the Maytide
      Without is working His will.

Without are the wind and the wall-flowers,
      The leaves and the nests and the rain,
And in all of them God is making
      His beautiful purpose plain.

But I wait in a horror of strangeness—
      A tool on His workshop floor,
Worn to the butt, and banished
      His hand for evermore.

L

So let me hence as one
Whose part in the world has been dreamed out
    and done :
One that hath fairly earned and spent
In pride of heart and jubilance of blood
Such wages, be they counted bad or good,
As Time, the old taskmaster, was moved to pay ;
And, having warred and suffered, and passed on
Those gifts the Arbiters preferred and gave,
Fare, grateful and content,
Down the dim way
Whereby races innumerable have gone,
Into the silent universe of the grave.

Grateful for what hath been—
For what my hand hath done, mine eyes have
    seen,
My heart been privileged to know ;

With all my lips in love have brought
To lips that yearned in love to them, and wrought
In the way of wrath, and pity, and sport, and
    song :
Content, this miracle of being alive
Dwindling, that I, thrice weary of worst and best,
May shed my duds, and go
From right and wrong,
And, ceasing to regret, and long, and strive,
Accept the past, and be for ever at rest.

FINALE

Schizzando ma con sentimento

A sigh sent wrong,
A kiss that goes astray,
A sorrow the years endlong—-
So they say.

So let it be—
Come the sorrow, the kiss, the sigh!
They are life, dear life, all three,
And we die.

WORTHING, 1899-1901.

II

LONDON TYPES

(To S. S. P.*)*

K

I

BUS-DRIVER

He 's called *The General* from the brazen craft
And dash with which he *sneaks a bit of road*
And all its fares ; challenged, or chafed, or chaffed,
Back-answers of the newest he 'll explode ;
He reins his horses with an air ; he treats
With scoffing calm whatever powers there be ;
He *gets it straight*, puts *a bit on*, and meets
His losses with both *lip* and *£ s. d.* ;
He arrogates a special taste in *short* ;
Is loftily grateful for a flagrant *smoke* ;
At all the smarter housemaids winks his court,
And taps them for half-crowns ; being *stoney-broke*,
    Lives lustily ; is ever *on the make* ;
    And hath, I fear, none other gods but *Fake*.

II

LIFE-GUARDSMAN

Joy of the Milliner, Envy of the Line,
Star of the Parks, jack-booted, sworded, helmed,
He sits between his holsters, solid of spine;
Nor, as it seems, though *WESTMINSTER* were
    whelmed,
With the great globe, in earthquake and eclipse,
Would he and his charger cease from mounting
    guard,
This Private in the Blues, nor would his lips
Move, though his gorge with throttled oaths were
    charred !
He wears his inches weightily, as he wears
His old-world armours; and with his port and
    pride,
His sturdy graces and enormous airs,
He towers, in speech his Colonel countrified,
    A triumph, waxing statelier year by year,
    Of British blood, and bone, and beef, and
        beer.

III

HAWKER

Far out of bounds he 's figured—in a race
Of West-End traffic pitching to his loss.
But if you 'd see him in his proper place,
Making the *browns* for *bub* and *grub* and *doss*,
Go East among the merchants and their men,
And where the press is noisiest, and the tides
Of trade run highest and widest, there and then
You shall behold him, edging with equal strides
Along the kerb ; hawking in either hand
Some artful nothing made of twine and tin,
Cardboard and foil and bits of rubber band :
Some penn'orth of wit-in-fact that, with a grin,
 The careful City marvels at, and buys
 For nurselings in the Suburbs to despise !

IV

BEEF-EATER

His beat lies knee-high through a dust of story—
A dust of terror and torture, grief and crime;
Ghosts that are ENGLAND'S wonder, and shame,
    and glory
Throng where he walks, an antic of old time;
A sense of long immedicable tears
Were ever with him, could his ears but heed;
The stern *Hic Jacets* of our bloodiest years
Are for his reading, had he eyes to read,
But here, where CROOKBACK raged, and CRANMER
    trimmed,
And MORE and STRAFFORD faced the axe's proving,
He shows that Crown the desperate Colonel
    nimmed,
Or simply keeps the Country Cousin moving,
    Or stays such Cockney pencillers as would
      shame
    The wall where some dead Queen hath traced
      her name.

v

SANDWICH-MAN

An ill March noon ; the flagstones gray with dust ;
An all-round east wind volleying straws and grit ;
St. Martin's Steps, where every venomous gust
Lingers to buffet, or sneap, the passing cit ;
And in the gutter, squelching a rotten boot,
Draped in a wrap that, modish ten-year syne,
Partners, obscene with sweat and grease and soot,
A horrible hat, that once was just as fine ;
The drunkard's mouth a-wash for something
    drinkable,
The drunkard's eye alert for casual *toppers*,
The drunkard's neck stooped to a lot scarce
    thinkable,
A living, crawling blazoning of Hot-Coppers,
    He trails his mildews towards a Kingdom-
      Come
    Compact of *sausage-and-mash* and *two-o'-rum* !

VI

'LIZA

'*LIZA's old man*'s perhaps a little *shady*,
'*LIZA's old woman*'s prone to *booze* and cringe ;
But '*LIZA* deems herself *a perfect lady*,
And proves it in her feathers and her fringe.
For '*LIZA* has a *bloke* her heart to cheer,
With *pearlies* and a *barrer* and a *jack*,
So all the vegetables of the year
Are duly represented on her back.
Her boots are sacrifices to her hats,
Which knock you speechless—*like a load of bricks !*
Her summer velvets dazzle *WANSTEAD FLATS*,
And cost, at times, a good eighteen-and-six.
      Withal, outside the gay and giddy whirl,
      '*LIZA*'s a stupid, straight, hard-working girl.

VII

'LADY'

Time, the old humourist, has a trick to-day
Of moving landmarks and of levelling down,
Till into Town the Suburbs edge their way,
And in the Suburbs you may scent the Town.
With *Mount St.* thus approaching *Muswell Hill*,
And *Clapham Common* marching with the *Mile*,
You get a *Hammersmith* that *fills the bill*,
A *Hampstead* with a serious sense of style.
So this fair creature, pictured in *The Row*,
As one of that 'gay adulterous world,'[1] whose round
Is by the *Serpentine*, as well would show,
And might, I deem, as readily be found
  On *Streatham's Hill*, or *Wimbledon's*, or
   where
Brixtonian kitchens lard the late-dining air.

[1] Wilfrid Blunt.

L

VIII

BLUECOAT BOY

So went our boys when *EDWARD SIXTH*, the King,
Chartered *CHRIST'S HOSPITAL*, and died.   And so
Full fifteen generations in a string
Of heirs to his bequest have had to go.
Thus *CAMDEN* showed, and *BARNES*, and *STILLING-
    FLEET*,
And *RICHARDSON*, that bade our *LOVELACE* be ;
The little *ELIA* thus in *NEWGATE STREET* ;
Thus to his *GENEVIEVE* young *S. T. C.*
With thousands else that, wandering up and down,
Quaint, privileged, liked and reputed well,
Made the great School a part of *LONDON TOWN*
Patent as *PAUL'S* and vital as *BOW BELL* :
    The old School nearing exile, day by day,
    To certain clay - lands somewhere *HORSHAM*
    way.

IX

MOUNTED POLICE

Army Reserve ; a worshipper of *Bobs*,
With whom he stripped the smock from *Canda-
        har;*
Neat as his mount, that neatest among cobs ;
Whenever pageants pass, or meetings are,
He moves conspicuous, vigilant, severe,
With his Light Cavalry hand and seat and look,
A living type of Order, in whose sphere
Is room for neither *Hooligan* nor *Hook*.
For in his shadow, wheresoe'er he ride,
Paces, all eye and hardihood and grip,
The dreaded *Crusher*, might in his every stride
And right materialized girt at his hip ;
        And they, that shake to see these twain go by,
        Feel that the *Tec*, that plain-clothes Terror,
            is nigh.

x

NEWS-BOY

Take any station, pavement, circus, corner,
Where men their styles of print may call or choose,
And there—ten times more *on it* than *Jack
        Horner*—
There shall you find him swathed in sheets of news.
Nothing can stay the placing of his wares—
Not bus, nor cab, nor dray !   The very *Slop*,
That imp of power, is powerless !   Ever he dares,
And, daring, lands his public neck and crop.
Even the many-tortured London ear,
The much-enduring, loathes his *Speeshul* yell,
His shriek of *Winnur !*   But his dart and leer
And poise are irresistible.   *Pall Mall*
        Joys in him, and *Mile End* ; for his vocation
        Is to purvey the stuff of conversation.

XI

DRUM-MAJOR

Who says *Drum-Major* says a man of mould,
Shaking the meek earth with tremendous tread,
And pacing still, a triumph to behold,
Of his own spine at least two yards ahead !
Attorney, grocer, surgeon, broker, duke—
His calling may be anything, who comes
Into a room, his presence a rebuke
To the dejected, as the pipes and drums
Inspired his port !—who mounts his office stairs
As though he led great armies to the fight !
His bulk itself's pure genius, and he wears
His avoirdupois with so much fire and spright
    That, though the creature stands but five
        feet five,
    You take him for the tallest He alive.

XII

FLOWER-GIRL

There's never a delicate nurseling of the year
But our huge *LONDON* hails it, and delights
To wear it on her breast or at her ear,
Her days to colour and make sweet her nights.
Crocus and daffodil and violet,
Pink, primrose, valley-lily, clove-carnation,
Red rose and white rose, wall-flower, mignonette,
The daisies all—these be her recreation,
Her gaudies these!   And forth from *DRURY LANE*,
Trapesing in any of her whirl of weathers,
Her flower-girls foot it, honest and hoarse and
        vain,
All boot and little shawl and wilted feathers :
        Of populous corners right advantage taking,
        And, where they squat, endlessly posy-making.

XIII

BARMAID

Though, if you ask her name, she says *ELISE*,
Being plain *ELIZABETH*, e'en let it pass,
And own that, if her aspirates take their ease,
She ever makes a point, in washing glass,
Handling the engine, turning taps for *tots*,
And countering change, and scorning what men
     say,
Of posing as a dove among the pots,
Nor often gives her dignity away.
Her head's a work of art, and, if her eyes
Be tired and ignorant, she has a waist;
Cheaply the Mode she shadows ; and she tries
From penny novels to amend her taste;
    And, having mopped the zinc for certain
      years,
    And faced the gas, she fades and disappears.

The Artist muses at his ease,
Contented that his work is done.
And smiling—smiling!—as he sees
His crowd collecting, one by one.
Alas! his travail's but begun!
None, none can keep the years in line,
And what to Ninety-Eight is fun
May raise the gorge of Ninety-Nine!

MUSWELL HILL, 1898.

III

THREE PROLOGUES

M

I

BEAU AUSTIN

By W. E. Henley and R. L. Stevenson,
Haymarket Theatre, November 3, 1890.

Spoken by Mr. TREE in the character of Beau Austin.

'To all and singular,' as DRYDEN says,
We bring a fancy of those Georgian days,
Whose style still breathed a faint and fine perfume
Of old-world courtliness and old-world bloom :
When speech was elegant and talk was fit,
For slang had not been canonised as wit ;
When manners reigned, when breeding had the
    wall,
And Women—yes !—were ladies first of all ;
When Grace was conscious of its gracefulness,
And man—though Man !—was not ashamed to
    dress.
A brave formality, a measured ease
Were his—and hers—whose effort was to please.
And to excel in pleasing was to reign,
And, if you sighed, never to sigh in vain.

But then, as now—it may be, something more—
Woman and man were human to the core.
The hearts that throbbed behind that brave attire
Burned with a plenitude of essential fire.
They too could risk, they also could rebel :
They could love wisely—they could love too well.
In that great duel of Sex, that ancient strife
Which is the very central fact of life,
They could—and did—engage it breath for breath,
They could—and did—get wounded unto death.
As at all times since time for us began
Woman was truly woman, man was man,
And joy and sorrow were as much at home
In trifling TUNBRIDGE as in mighty ROME.

Dead—dead and done with !   Swift from shine
        to shade
The roaring generations flit and fade.
To this one, fading, flitting, like the rest,
We come to proffer—be it worst or best—
A sketch, a shadow, of one brave old time ;
A hint of what it might have held sublime ;
A dream, an idyll, call it what you will,
Of man still Man, and woman—Woman still !

II

RICHARD SAVAGE

By J. M. Barrie and H. B. Marriott Watson,
Criterion Theatre, April 16, 1891.

To other boards for pun and song and dance !
Our purpose is an essay in romance :
An old-world story where such old-world facts
As hate and love and death, through four swift
     acts—
Not without gleams and glances, hints and cues,
From the dear bright eyes of the Comic Muse !—
So shine and sound that, as we fondly deem,
They may persuade you to accept our dream :
Our own invention, mainly—though we take,
Somewhat for art but most for interest's sake
One for our hero who goes wandering still
In the long shadow of PARNASSUS HILL ;
Scarce within eyeshot ; but his tragic shade
Compels that recognition due be made,
When he comes knocking at the student's door,
Something as poet, if as blackguard more.

Poet and blackguard.   Of the first—how much?
As to the second, in quite perfect touch
With folly and sorrow, even shame and crime,
He lived the grief and wonder of his time !
Marked for reproaches from his life's beginning ;
Extremely sinned against as well as sinning ;
Hack, spendthrift, starveling, duellist in turn ;
Too cross to cherish yet too fierce to spurn ;
Begrimed with ink or brave with wine and
    blood ;
Spirit of fire and manikin of mud ;
Now shining clear, now fain to starve and skulk ;
Star of the cellar, pensioner of the bulk ;
At once the child of passion and the slave ;
Brawling his way to an unhonoured grave——
That was *DICK SAVAGE !*   Yet, ere his ghost we
    raise
For these more decent and less desperate days,
It may be well and seemly to reflect
That, howbeit of so prodigal a sect,
Since it was his to call until the end
Our greatest, wisest Englishman his friend,
'Twere all-too fatuous if we cursed and scorned
The strange, wild creature *JOHNSON* loved and
    mourned.

Nature is but the oyster—Art's the pearl :
Our *Dick* is neither sycophant nor churl.
Not as he was but as he might have been
Had the Unkind Gods been poets of the scene,
Fired with our fancy, shaped and tricked anew
To touch your hearts with love, your eyes with
    rue,
He stands or falls, ere he these boards depart,
Not as dead Nature but as living Art.

III

ADMIRAL GUINEA

By *W. E. Henley* and *R. L. Stevenson*,
Avenue Theatre, Monday, November 29, 1897.

Spoken by Miss ELIZABETH ROBINS.

Once was an Age, an Age of blood and gold,
An Age of shipmen scoundrelly and bold—
BLACKBEARD and AVORY, SINGLETON, ROBERTS, KIDD :
An Age which seemed, the while it rolled its quid,
Brave with adventure and doubloons and crime,
Rum and the Ebony Trade : when, time on time,
Real Pirates, right Sea-Highwaymen, could mock
The carrion strung at EXECUTION DOCK ;
And the trim Slaver, with her raking rig,
Her cloud of sails, her spars superb and trig,
Held, in a villainous ecstasy of gain,
Her musky course from BENIN to the MAIN,
And back again for niggers :
                              When, in fine,
Some thought that EDEN bloomed across the Line,
And some, like COWPER'S NEWTON, lived to tell
That through those parallels ran the road to Hell.

Once was a pair of Friends, who loved to
    chance
Their feet in any by-way of Romance :
They, like two vagabond schoolboys, unafraid
Of stark impossibilities, essayed
To make these Penitent and Impenitent Thieves,
These *PEWS* and *GAUNTS*, each man of them with
    his sheaves
Of humour, passion, cruelty, tyranny, life,
Fit shadows for the boards ; till in the strife
Of dream with dream, their Slaver-Saint came true,
And their Blind Pirate, their resurgent *PEW*
(A figure of deadly farce in his new birth),
Tap-tapped his way from *ORCUS* back to earth ;
And so, their Lover and his Lass made one,
In their best prose this *Admiral* here was done.

One of this Pair sleeps till the crack of doom
Where the great ocean-rollers plunge and boom :
The other waits and wonders what his Friend,
Dead now, and deaf, and silent, were the end
Revealed to his rare spirit, would find to say
If you, his lovers, loved him for this Play.

N

IV

EPICEDIA

TWO DAYS

(February 15—*September* 28, 1894)

To V. G.

THAT day we brought our Beautiful One to lie
In the green peace within your gates, he came
To give us greeting, boyish and kind and shy,
And, stricken as we were, we blessed his name :
Yet, like the Creature of Light that had been ours,
Soon of the sweet Earth disinherited,
He too must join, even with the Year's old flowers,
The unanswering generations of the Dead.
So stand we friends for you, who stood our friend
Through him that day ; for now through him you
    know
That though where love was, love is till the end,
Love, turned of death to longing, like a foe,
    Strikes : when the ruined heart goes forth to
      crave
    Mercy of the high, austere, unpitying Grave.

IN MEMORIAM

THOMAS EDWARD BROWN

(*Ob. October* 30, 1897)

He looked half-parson and half-skipper: a quaint,
Beautiful blend, with blue eyes good to see,
And old-world whiskers.   You found him cynic,
    saint,
Salt, humourist, Christian, poet; with a free,
Far-glancing, luminous utterance ; and a heart
Large as ST. FRANCIS'S : withal a brain
Stored with experience, letters, fancy, art,
And scored with runes of human joy and pain.
Till six-and-sixty years he used his gift,
His gift unparalleled, of laughter and tears,
And left the world a high-piled, golden drift
Of verse: to grow more golden with the years,
    Till the Great Silence fallen upon his ways
    Break into song, and he that had Love have
    Praise.

IN *MEMORIAM*

GEORGE WARRINGTON STEEVENS

London, December 10, 1869.
Ladysmith, January 15, 1900.

We cheered you forth—brilliant and kind and brave.
　Under your country's triumphing flag you fell.
It floats, true Heart, over no dearer grave—
　Brave and brilliant and kind, hail and farewell !

LAST POST

The day's high work is over and done,
And these no more will need the sun :
Blow, you bugles of *ENGLAND*, blow !
These are gone whither all must go,
Mightily gone from the field they won.
So in the workaday wear of battle,
Touched to glory with *GOD'S* own red,
Bear we our chosen to their bed.
Settle them lovingly where they fell,
In that good lap they loved so well ;
And, their deliveries to the dear *LORD* said,
And the last desperate volleys ranged and sped,
Blow, you bugles of *ENGLAND*, blow
Over the camps of her beaten foe—
Blow glory and pity to the victor Mother,
Sad, O, sad in her sacrificial dead !

Labour, and love, and strife, and mirth,
They gave their part in this goodly Earth—

Blow, you bugles of *ENGLAND*, blow!—
That her Name as a sun among stars might glow,
Till the dusk of Time, with honour and worth :
That, stung by the lust and the pain of battle,
The One Race ever might starkly spread,
And the One Flag eagle it overhead !
In a rapture of wrath and faith and pride,
Thus they felt it, and thus they died ;
So to the Maker of homes, to the Giver of bread,
For whose dear sake their triumphing souls they
      shed,
Blow, you bugles of *ENGLAND*, blow,
Though you break the heart of her beaten foe,
Glory and praise to the everlasting Mother,
Glory and peace to her lovely and faithful dead !

IN MEMORIAM

REGINAE DILECTISSIMAE VICTORIAE

(*May* 24, 1819—*January* 22, 1901)

Sceptre and orb and crown,
High ensigns of a sovranty containing
The beauty and strength and state of half a World,
Pass from her, and she fades
Into the old, inviolable peace.

I

She had been ours so long
She seemed a piece of ENGLAND : spirit and blood
And message ENGLAND'S self,
Home-coloured, ENGLAND in look and deed and
    dream ;
Like the rich meadows and woods, the serene
    rivers,
And sea-charmed cliffs and beaches, that still bring

A rush of tender pride to the heart
That beats in *ENGLAND'S* airs to *ENGLAND'S* ends :
August, familiar, irremovable,
Like the good stars that shine
In the good skies that only *ENGLAND* knows :
So that we held it sure
GOD'S aim, *GOD'S* will, *GOD'S* way,
When Empire from her footstool, realm on realm,
Spread, even as from her notable womb
Sprang line on line of Kings ;
For she was *ENGLAND—ENGLAND* and our
    Queen.

II

O, she was ours !   And she had aimed
And known and done the best
And highest in time : greatly rejoiced,
Ruled greatly, greatly endured.   Love had been
    hers,
And widowhood, glory and grief, increase
In wisdom and power and pride,
Dominion, honour, children, reverence :
So that, in peace and war

Innumerably victorious, she lay down
To die in a world renewed,
Cleared, in her luminous umbrage beautified
For Man, and changing fast
Into so gracious an inheritance
As Man had never dared
Imagine. Think, when she passed,
Think what a pageant of immortal acts,
Done in the unapproachable face
Of Time by the high, transcending human mind,
Shone and acclaimed
And triumphed in her advent!   Think of the
    ghosts,
Think of the mighty ghosts : soldiers and priests,
Artists and captains of discovery,
GOD'S chosen, His adventurers up the heights
Of thought and deed—how many of them that
    led
The forlorn hopes of the World !—
Her peers and servants, made the air
Of her death-chamber glorious! Think how they
    thronged
About her bed, and with what pride
They took this sister-ghost
Tenderly into the night !   O, think—

And, thinking, bow the head
In sorrow, but in the reverence that makes
The strong man stronger—this true maid,
True wife, true mother, tried and found
An hundred times true steel,
This unforgettable woman was your Queen !

III

Tears for her—tears !   Tears and the mighty rites
Of an everlasting and immense farewell,
England, green heart of the world, and you,
Dear demi-*Englands*, far-away isles of home,
Where the old speech is native, and the old flag
Floats, and the old irresistible call,
The watch-word of so many ages of years,
Makes men in love
With toil for the race, and pain, and peril, and
        death !
Tears, and the dread, tremendous dirge
Of her brooding battleships, and hosts
Processional, with trailing arms ; the plaint—
Measured, enormous, terrible—of her guns ;
The slow, heart-breaking throb

Of bells ; the trouble of drums ; the blare
Of mourning trumpets ; the discomforting pomp
Of silent crowds, black streets, and banners-royal
Obsequious !   Then, these high things done,
Rise, heartened of your passion !   Rise to the
    height
Of her so lofty life !   Kneel, if you must ;
But, kneeling, win to those great altitudes
On which she sought and did
Her clear, supernal errand unperturbed !
Let the new memory
Be as the old, long love !   So, when the hour
Strikes, as it must, for valour of heart,
Virtue, and patience, and unblenching hope,
And the inflexible resolve
That, come the World in arms,
This breeder of nations, ENGLAND, keeping the seas
Hers as from GOD, shall in the sight of GOD
Stand justified of herself
Wherever her unretreating bugles blow !
Remember that she lived
That this magnificent Power might still perdure—
Your friend, your passionate servant, counsellor,
    Queen.

IV

Be that your chief of mourning—that!—
ENGLAND, O Mother, and you,
The daughter Kingdoms born and reared
Of ENGLAND'S travail and sweet blood;
And never will you lands,
The live Earth over and round,
Wherethrough for sixty royal and radiant years
Her drum-tap made the dawns
English—Never will you
So fittingly and well have paid your debt
Of grief and gratitude to the souls
That sink in ENGLAND'S harness into the dream :
' I die for ENGLAND'S sake, and it is well' :
As now to this valiant, wonderful piece of earth,
To which the assembling nations bare the head,
And bend the knee,
In absolute veneration—once your Queen.

Sceptre and orb and crown,
High ensigns of a sovranty empaling
The glory and love and praise of a whole half-world,
Fall from her, and, preceding, she departs
Into the old, indissoluble Peace.

EPILOGUE

Into a land
Storm-wrought, a place of quakes, all thunder-
    scarred,
Helpless, degraded, desolate,
Peace, the White Angel, comes.
Her eyes are as a mother's.   Her good hands
Are comforting, and helping ; and her voice
Falls on the heart, as, after Winter, Spring
Falls on the World, and there is no more pain.
And, in her influence, hope returns, and life,
And the passion of endeavour : so that, soon,
The idle ports are insolent with keels ;
The stithies roar, and the mills thrum
With energy and achievement ; weald and wold
Exult ; the cottage-garden teems
With innocent hues and odours ; boy and girl
Mate prosperously ; there are sweet women to kiss ;
There are good women to breed.   In a golden fog,

A large, full-stomached faith in kindliness
All over the world, the nation, in a dream
Of money and love and sport, hangs at the paps
Of well-being, and so
Goes fattening, mellowing, dozing, rotting down
Into a rich deliquium of decay.

Then, if the Gods be good,
Then, if the Gods be other than mischievous,
Down from their footstools, down
With a million-throated shouting, swoops and
     storms
War, the Red Angel, the Awakener,
The Shaker of Souls and Thrones ; and at her heel
Trail grief, and ruin, and shame !
The woman weeps her man, the mother her son,
The tenderling its father.   In wild hours,
A people, haggard with defeat,
Asks if there be a God ; yet sets its teeth,
Faces calamity, and goes into the fire
Another than it was.   And in wild hours
A people, roaring ripe
With victory, rises, menaces, stands renewed,
Sheds its old piddling aims,

P

Approves its virtue, puts behind itself
The comfortable dream, and goes,
Armoured and militant,
New-pithed, new-souled, new-visioned, up the
    steeps
To those great altitudes, whereat the weak
Live not.   But only the strong
Have leave to strive, and suffer, and achieve.

WORTHING, 1901.

Printed by T. and A. CONSTABLE, Printers to His Majesty
at the Edinburgh University Press

LaVergne, TN USA
27 May 2010
184148LV00001B/158/A